The Ringing Tones
of an
Ancient Calling

With Best Wishes.

To Ann.

Ham. David A Balloch

Lass Greet to the

City of Norwich

The Ringing Tones of an Ancient Calling

"Being the History of Bellmen / Town Criers in The City of Norwich and The Borough of Great Yarmouth"

by

David A. Bullock
Town Crier to The City of Norwich

Acknowledgements

The author wishes to thank the staff of both Gt. Yarmouth and Norwich Reference Libraries for their help in the research into this book and Brian Collins for the photographs.

Dedication

To my wife Irene.

ISBN 0 900616 46 6

Printed and published by
Geo. R. Reeve Ltd., Damgate, Wymondham, Norfolk.

CONTENTS

"My thanks to all, for your support
As the years unfold,
As we 'cry' your messages, in sunshine, rain and cold,
To 'cry' unto an empty street
Would be a pointless task,
So when you hear our bell and shout
This is all we ask
Stay awhile and gather round to listen to our call
Our only purpose thereabouts
Is to entertain you all."

INTRODUCTION

I suspect there has always been a Town Crier, or Bellman, ever since man started to communicate with man, especially with the advent of states and empires, when the rulers of such wished to communicate their decrees to the populace of their far-flung domains, although there are no clear definitions of the beginnings of town crying.

Messengers in Greece and Rome ran from town to town crying proclamations and decrees from their rulers to the people in the square.

Stentor was a Greek warrior in the Trojan War, whose voice was said to be as powerful as fifty voices of other men. Hence the word 'stentorian'; a word liberally used by Victorian writers to describe Bellmen and Town Criers in their day.

[1] "From 396 BC onwards, the games in Greece were opened by a contest for heralds (Town Criers) and trumpeters. This probably followed immediately after the ritual inauguration and was held to decide which trumpeter was to give the signal for the start of the various events and which herald was to proclaim the judges' verdict." (Much like the Town Crier competitions held now).

One would assume that Greek heralds would be athletic and fleet of foot, as I cannot imagine anything more risky than the following:-

[2] "When a war had been decided upon between Greek states, hostilities did not commence until the herald, whose person was sacrosanct, had announced the severing of relationships in a solemn and formal declaration. It was this same herald who, if things went badly, would bear proposals of truce or armistice to the enemy. A state of war between two states was defined as existing legally only after all relationships between them had been broken off by means of the heralds". One can imagine the two armies lined up facing each other with their spears bristling, worked to a frenzy by their generals, barely holding back, whilst the herald cries his proclamation of war. One hopes they gave him time to quit the field before hostilities commenced.

1 Olympia — Gods, Artists and Athletes by Ludwig Drees.
2 Daily Life in Greece at the Time of Pericles by Robert Flacelière.

In the British Isles the post of Bellman/Town Crier goes back to the twelfth/thirteenth centuries. There is a record of a Town Crier in Marlborough in 1204.

In 1272 in Norwich, a Town Crier with his bell, is mentioned in a Bull of Pope Gregory concerning the riots at the Cathedral.

In one part of the Bayeux Tapestry, there are two Bellman pictured under the body of King Edmund as he is being carried to Westminster Abbey. These could be 'skellat' Bellman who announced deaths and funerals and were usually ecclesiastical Bellmen.

In the early days of the calling in this country Town Criers and Bellmen were different entities.

A Town Crier was usually mentioned in the Charter of their respective towns, elected by the court leet and performed numerous functions within the court. The Bellman was usually a lesser mortal, not usually mentioned in the Charter. However, over the centuries, the two have become synonymous with the 'crying' of messages of all sorts.

From the sixteenth to the twentieth century, there has been many variations of livery or uniform. In some cases, no uniform at all. Most of today's Town Criers have civic or historical uniforms, copies of the mid-eighteenth century.

With the ringing of his bell, the Town Crier/Bellman commences his cry with "Oyez! Oyez! Oyez!" (from the old French meaning "Hear Ye") and concludes with "God Save The Queen", or, of course, King, when appropriate.

There are over a hundred Town Criers in great Britain today and I urge the reader to support them as part of our colourful heritage and history.

I hope that all who read this little offering derive as much pleasure from it as I did in compiling it.

NORWICH
Norfolk

*Eastern Daily Press
Saturday, 23rd October,
1926
Article by George A.
Stephen F.L.A. Part I
*a translation of which
forms an appendix to
Mr. Walter Rye's article
on "riot between the
monks and citizens of
Norwich in 1272",
published in his Norfolk
Antiquarian Miscellany
Volume 2 1883.
Town Life in the 15th
Century by Mrs. J.R.
Green
Publishers: Macmillan &
Co. 1894
Volume II
(Common Council of
Norwich)
Page 384.*

1272   Crier

"The earliest reference to a Crier or Bellman in Norwich which I have been able to trace, is that in a Bull of Pope Gregory issued in 1272*. This states that members of the commonalty who had completed their twelfth year were "summoned by the voice of the Crier and the sound of the bell for the utter extermination of the same monastery".

1385   Bellman

"In Norwich a Guild of Saint George was founded in 1385 as a fraternity with the usual religious colour and a Bellman "going each Monday about in the city remembering and praying for the souls of the brethren and sisters of the said Guild, that be passed to God's mercy."

*Eastern Daily Press
Saturday, 23rd October,
1926
Article by George A.
Stephen F.L.A. Part I
Composition printed in the
records of the City of
Norwich
Volume I (1906)*

1415   Bellman

Civic records of Norwich prove that an official Bellman was appointed in 1415. In that year a composition was agreed to for the purpose of carrying out the provisions of the Charter of Henry IV dated 1404. This composition provided that the whole assembly should chose the "Recordour, Belleman and Dykkepere".

1474/86   John Gobet   Bellman
Belleman was paid 8s.

*Eastern Daily Press
City Chamberlain's
Accounts. Also "Index To
Norwich City Officers
1453–1835", edited by
Timothy Howes.*

1489/98   William John Buston   Bellman
Belman for his livery this year 7s.8d.
(Blodij Coloris)

1544   John Basse   Bellman
34–35 Henry VIII The Bedell, John
Basse, for his livery this year 6s.8d.
The Bellman for his wages 6s.8d.

1580/81   Geffreye Empson   Bellman
To Geffreye Empson, Bellman, for the
whoale yeres fee 6s.8d.

Eastern Daily Press

1666   Bellman
21st July — The Bellman to proclaim
that no tradesman or shopkeeper do
refuse to take any farthings than of their
own stamp upon the penalty of being
proceeded against according to law.

Eastern Daily Press

1674/5   Bellman
16th January — John Whyar sent up a
note under his hand to have the Bellman
proclaim that no person do trust his wife
for any goods or money.

Eastern Daily Press

Eastern Daily Press	1677	Bellman

19th September — Bellman to proclaim that no person presume to take tobacco in the streets by day or night and that no carter whatsoever do ride upon the tybbs or in the body of the cart, but that he drives his cart on foot.

Eastern Daily Press	1678	Bellman

13th April 1678 — Dyke of London, Clockmaker, desired leave of court to decleorie his wife by the Bellman, she being a very idle and expensive person, running her husband in debt in several places. Leave granted.

Eastern Daily Press	1678	Bellman

9th November — the Bellman is to proclaim in the market at high noon that in respect of next Wednesday's feast there shall be no market, that shops be shut up and no carts up and down the streets.

Eastern Daily Press	1679	Bellman

15th November — Bellman to proclaim in the usual places the three notes read today in court for transport of such persons 'as are willing' to Barbados and Jamaica from Yarmouth.

1679/80   Bellman   *Eastern Daily Press*

6th March — Bellman to give notice that
no person shall set any carts on the north
side of the market cross, but with wheels
in the channel right against that part of
the market called The Walk. Clerk of
the market to provide forms, stools and
to charge a penny a day.

1681   Bellman   *Eastern Daily Press*

17th September — E.D.W. Cooke to buy
a barrow and shovel for the cross keeper
and the said cross keeper to take up the
muck in a cart which shall be made by
inhabitants dwelling in the market,
which is to be kept in tubs or buckets till
the cart comes, which shall be every
Monday and the Bellman to give notice
hereof publicly.

1687   Bellman   *Eastern Daily Press*

20th August — Proclamation to be made
by the Bellman straitly charging and
commanding that all manner of persons
within the city and county mind their
respective business and not resort in
companies before the King's Head Gate
in the market or before the Guard
House, or in any other place whereby to
affront any of His Majesty's soldiers
quartered in this city etc.

1780/1804 Nathaniel Eastaugh Bellman

The earliest address of a Norwich Bellman which I (George A. Stephen) have traced is that issued in 1780 by Nathaniel Eastaugh during his first year of office. In Eastaugh's first address above a woodcut of the Bellman herein reproduced is the title "A new copy of verses humbly presented to the Right Worshipful The Mayor, Alderman, Sheriffs, common council men and the rest of my worthy masters and mistresses in the city of Norwich" by Nathaniel Eastaugh, Bellman 1780. The prologue reads — "let learned authors over generous wine, in lofty numbers make their verses shine, my lines in humble strains shall gently flow, and not my learning, but my duty shew, tho' judgement wanting fain I would impart, the simple dictates of an honest heart, then pray excuse your servant's want of skill, and kindly take the product of Hill Quill". Eastaugh's prologue is followed by stanzas on Christmas Day, New Year's Day, the Present War, The King, The Prince of Wales, The Right Worshipful The Mayor, The Aldermen, The Sheriffs, The Commons, my married masters, my married mistresses, the batchelors, the maidens followed by an epilogue.

Regarding the Mayor, Benjamin Day, he wrote:-

Great and generous Sir! May peace attend

And gracious heav'n its assistance lend,
To bless that year which to fair Norwich gave
A Mayor so just, so generous and so brave
Our Saxon ancestors indeed are prais'd
From having from a pile of ruins rais'd
Great Norfolk's capital, which now defies
All foreign and domestic enemies.
This truth with gratitude and joy I tell,
That you were Mayor when I received the bell.

For many years Eastaugh lived in Bethel Street. In 1783 he lived at No.4 and in 1801 at No.39. Apparently Eastaugh did not always walk on his rounds. In the prologue of his 1807 address he describes himself as "the cat'lani of Bellmen on horseback I sit!"

1804   John Buckle   Bellman   *Eastern Daily Press*

1805/1810 Nathaniel Eastaugh Bellman   *Eastern Daily Press*
"Except during the year, 1804, when John Buckle was the Bellman, Nathaniel Eastaugh, who was also one of the Mayor's beadles, held office continuously until March 22nd 1810 when he died in the Parish of St. Peter Mancroft, aged 57 years. His annual official fee was 13s.4d.

During the latter part of his life the cobbled streets must have been a source of great trouble and inconvenience to him because the 'Norfolk Chronicle' of 7th November 1807 contained the following announcement:- "Nathaniel Eastaugh, Bellman of Norwich, in gratitude for having had possession of the city bell for twenty-seven years (for one year only excepted) has liberally subscribed the sum of ten guineas towards the new pavement, he being at times unable through infirmity to walk over the old one.

Eastern Daily Press
Tuesday, 26th October,
1926
Part II

1810/1812   Anthony Bailey   Bellman
He succeeded Eastaugh and held office during the years 1810/12, 1816/17 and in 1822. He lived at St. Martin's Palace Plain and by trade was a cotton manufacturer. The woodcut which appeared on Eastaugh's address was used on Bailey's address until 1816.

Eastern Daily Press

1813/1815   Robert Juby   Bellman
He used the woodcut of the Bellman which illustrated the addresses of Eastaugh. I (George A. Stephen) have been unable to trace any particulars regarding Juby, but he may have been the Robert Juby, a weaver, who lived in St. Stephen's and whose name appeared in the Norwich Poll Book of 1818. As to who was the Bellman in the years 1819 1821 and 1823 I cannot say.

1816/1817   Anthony Bailey   Bellman   *Eastern Daily Press*
1817 Bailey used different woodcut on his address.

1818   Robert Juby   Bellman   *Eastern Daily Press*

1822   Anthony Bailey   Bellman   *Eastern Daily Press*

1824/1826 Nathaniel Eastaugh II Bellman   *Eastern Daily Press*
A second Nathaniel Eastaugh was appointed Bellman in 1824. He also held office in 1825-6, 1830 and 1832-5. He was the son of Nathaniel Eastaugh, probably the former Bellman of that name: for his addresses he used the same woodcut used by Anthony Bailey, probably because he employed the same printers, Matchett and Stevenson, of The Market Place, Norwich.

1827/1829   James Berry   Bellman   *Eastern Daily Press*
He was Bellman in 1827/29, 1831 and 1836/56. At first he illustrated his addresses with the woodcut formerly used by Eastaugh, probably because he employed the same printers, Bacon & Kinnebrook. Kept Red Lion in St. Andrews, Norwich.

1830   Nathaniel Eastaugh   Bellman   *Eastern Daily Press*

1831   James Berry   Bellman   *Eastern Daily Press*
In the address of 1831 he had a new woodcut, a Bellman wearing a three-cornered hat and a long coat with city arms. In his right hand is a bell and in his left a lantern, while at his feet is a dog.

In 1831, as now economy was expected to be the watchword of the council, the verse relating to the common council being as follows:-

To you our local Parliament –
The commons of our court,
Whose votes are doubtless fairly meant
To gain a good report
And such report you'll have from me
And from each candid man
As long as we can clearly see
Economy's your plan.

Eastern Daily Press

1832/1835 Nathaniel Eastaugh Bellman
In the prologue to his address for Christmas 1834, he boldly asked for a Christmas gift from his patrons:-

Me, City Bellman, dogg'rel rhymes to write,
Awake my muse such verse inspire,
As well may suit a Bellman's lyre,
For me, the humblest of thy throng
That strive to paint their thoughts in song
To nought I ever make pretence,
But artless phrase and common sense
Give me but these to deck my lay
And my heart's gratitude convey,
The merits of my friends I'll tell
In verse harmonious as my bell
Now I beat my annual round
Among my numerous friends are found
Some who will nobly throw me down
A heart enlivening fair half-crown

While others do but sixpence give
Yet sixpence I with thanks receive
But O! may none be found unwilling
To bless me with a splendid shilling".
Some of the stanzas in a few of Eastagh's
addresses and also some of those of his
successors are either the same or very
similar. Perhaps because the different
Bellmen employed the same rhymester.
He died 16th January, 1845 and was
buried in St. Stephen's Churchyard.

1836/1856   James Berry   Bellman   *Eastern Daily Press*
In 1836 and subsequently a different
woodblock was used. Probably the
illustration was intended as a portrayal
of himself in a long coat with the city
arms and a tall hat, with a bell in his right
hand, standing in front of The Guildhall.
The address of 1836 shows that the
duties of the Norwich Bellman had
increased and embraced cries of great
diversity, as witness the prologue:-
"The muse, good sirs, has dar'd to
wing her flight
To teach your humble servant what to
write
For though a Bellman, yet I am no
poet,
But this I need not say for all must
know it

My business is aloud to tell my tales
Of losses, fish and also public sales
Amusements too, I oft proclaim aloud
And with my tales, amuse the
gathering crowd
Sometimes I cry of birds and beasts of
prey
And little urchins who have lost their
way
Sometimes of naughty wives who've
left their spouses
And gone to live in other people's
houses
All this you'll say, perhaps is very well
But while I live I hope to bear the bell.

Eastern Daily Press

1857/1877   Josiah Berry   Bellman
In 1857 Josiah Berry, a Freeman of the City, succeeded his father, James Berry, and retained the bell continuously for twenty years until he died on April 3rd, 1877 aged sixty years. The addresses for the years 1857–1864 bear the name 'Josiah Berry' while those for the years 1865–1876 have 'Josiah Bush Berry', but evidently they were all issued by the same man, because Harrod's Directory of Norfolk and Norwich for the year 1863 gives the full name 'Josiah Bush Berry', Bellman, St. Benedict's Plain. In Kelly's Post Office Directory of Norfolk for 1875, he was described as Town Crier and Bailiff to the Corn Exchange, Pottergate Street. His address of 1859 and his subsequent addresses had a

woodcut, probably of himself, standing in front of the Guildhall in his official dress, a frock coat with the city arms and a top hat, the bell being under his left arm.

Until 1867 Berry received from the corporation, the annual fee of 13s.4d., which sum had been paid yearly for over three hundred years. In 1868 the fee was increased to £5 13s.4d.

The copies of the addresses for 1865 and 1866 have interesting and significant notes apparently in contemporary handwriting. The note on the earlier address reads, "The Poetry by Richardson, late schoolmaster of Norwich gaol and poet to the corporation for the last twenty-eight years". The later note is as follows, "Poetry by Richardson, who has composed for the Bellman for the last twenty years".

1835   Nathaniel Eastaugh II   Bellman (Under other officers) Bellman and Beadle yearly salary of 13s.4d. and fees for crying.
Crier — not named in Charter.
Crier of the Court — 10s. a year salary and the usual fees at sessions and the Sheriff's Court.

Royal Commission on Municipal Corporations in England and Wales 1835
Appendix to first report Part IV 2459 2466

1877/1905   William Childerhouse

Bellman

Undoubtedly the most remarkable and celebrated Bellman of Norwich and, perhaps, of the whole country, in the latter half of the nineteenth century, was William Childerhouse, "the little man with the big voice", who is still vividly remembered by many citizens. Childerhouse was discovered by the late Mr. James Spilling, the Editor of the Eastern Daily Press, who recognised the value of his loud, deep voice, when he kept a shop in Alexandra Road and hawked "Stewkey" mussels and water "Creeses". He was employed to deliver copies of the Eastern Daily Press in the Heigham district. He began with the first issue on 10th October, 1870 and continued his job for about thirty years. Regarding him, the article on the Jubilee Commemmoration of the Eastern Daily Press (published in 1920) said "Hail, shine, blow or snow, he was with us every morning. The slush would fly from his heels, the rain would cascade from his ruinous tall hat and sodden his dundreary whiskers. The invariable burden of his song was "whatever you forget, don't forget the pay,por!"

For more than seven years he was a lay preacher at the Sprowston Baptist Chapel. He was appointed Bellman and sword bearer on 17th April, 1877 and held office continuously until his death in 1905. The obituary notice published in the Eastern Daily Press said of him:-

"Surcharged with activity and brimful of humour, always ready to give and take a jest, he was a general favourite and could truthfully boast that he had not a single enemy in the whole community. His sonorous voice, quaint official style and ready wit attracted visitors for a long period and a London journalist noticed a resemblance between him and a distinguished K.C. and described him as "exactly like Sir Edward Clarke in fancy dress costume".

Picture postcards of him were issued and sent all over the world.

His first address, dated 1877, began with three stanzas on "The Bellmanship Past and Present".

In days of yore, two centuries ago,
As in the verse of Herrick you may see
The Bellman every night went to and from,
To cry, "From noise of scare fires rest ye free."
For in the days when police were not,
A watchman's duty on the Bellman fell
His nightly rounds he went, and ne'er forgot
When lurid flames appeared to ring his bell.
Should e'er a thief abroad he chance to spy,
He boldly followed up the prowling knave

He knew right well he had no need to fly
E'en were the night as lonely as the grave
For he would summon all with son'rous
knell
By vig'rous using of his trusty bell
Not now the Bellman nightly has to
roam,
From ward to ward with lighted lamp
and bell
To see that cit'zens sleep undisturbed at
home
And yawning cry, "It's one o'clock! Alls
well".
That cry still lingers with the lonely night
Who right well watches Gurney's Golden
store
"Eleven o'clock, All's well" he cries each
night
And may he ne'er have cause to cry aught
more.
Not now does Bellman's voice or waking
bell
Of midnight fire proclaim the first alarm.
The police explode the thund'ring rocket
shell,
And strive our city old to save from harm.
When now are heard his voice and bell so
loud,
'Tis mostly day, and always mid a crowd.
At end of concert sweet, or festive ball
The Bellman's voice afar is heard aloud.
"The Mayor's carriage!" loudly does he
call
And straight it comes advancing from the
crowd.

With active movement, carriage door he
flings
Wide open, that the fare may quick
away.
Then loud again for humble cab he sings
And ladies smile their thanks — Ah!
Well-a-day!
But is this Bellman's work? some may
demand,
Aye, in good sooth, it is; 'Tis quickly
shown,
'Tis plain as digits are upon your hand.
The wonder is, the reason's not well
known,
Plain common sense alone us truly tells
The Bellman's the attendant of the
belles.

When the death of Josiah Berry was
reported to the Town Council in April
1877, a councillor suggested that a
Bellman was no longer required. In his
first address to his 'Patrons and
Patronesses', Childerhouse contested this
view and indicated the variety of his 'cries':
"Ladies and Gentlemen — the last eight
months have proved that the bell is not
what it was thought to be, a thing of the
past, for, since the time it was first set going
after my appointment, it has not ceased
day by day to ring out its note, the Bellman
who makes known his stentorophonic
power when favoured with your orders:-
consisting of losses and finds, sales public
and private, rinking, concerts sublime,
unique, bazaars, on the grand,

commissions from butchers and bakers, grocers and drapers, tailors and traders, etc. etc., brings grist to the mill of his employers and himself, for which he begs most respectfully to tender his sincerest thanks, while he intimates that he awaits further orders. Proud of his 'stentorophonic power' he referred to it in his address of 1889:-

A notice brief I wish to give,
Princes Street is where I live,
At number thirty-four,
At this address you'll always find,
The man who has a willing mind
Your notices to pour,
He gives his accents loud and clear
They're sure to fall upon the ear
Often they please full well
Up and down the streets he'll go
While people pass both to and fro
Sounding the ten pound bell
"Dear me," says one, "What a voice he's got
It echoes like a cannon-shot,
Of that none can complain."

Unlike his predecessor's addresses, which were always in verse, Childerhouse's addresses were principally in prose, with occasional stanzas. In his second address the paragraph 'to the council' contained a reference to the new wood paving:-

Your attention has been principally engaged in the improvement of the city. I may here mention one important advance viz. the wood pavement which I trust will be extended till 'petrified kidneys' are no longer known in our streets, so that the stentorian voice of the Bellman may be heard from Howlett's Corner to Gurney's Bank and from Tombland to Stump Cross, which will be a saving to the wear and tear of his lungs, as well as the tires of the wheels of the traps of our tradesmen".

To the popularity of the organ recitals of Dr. Bunnett, then city organist, he paid the following tribute in his address of 1884:-

The organ recitals by Dr. Bunnett
F.C.O.
Have taken, as the treasurer's figures show
I'm not ashamed to tell they're always grand
When human voices sound as if from pilgrim band.
The 'storm' piece always thrills thro' me
And so does the 'Chapel By The Sea!"

A fee charged by Childerhouse for 'crying' round the city was mentioned in his address of 1887:-

"My fee, says I, is half-a-crown,
For forty announcements in the town
But if I'm wanted more the twice
I make a difference in the price".

Childerhouse's last address, dated Christmas 1904 and the new Year 1905, concluded with a pious injunction:-

"We know not, we cannot tell
For whom, this year, will toll the bell
Many are gone whom we thought
In this year would still have wrought
The same old watchword 'Be Ye
Ready'
On life's seas, hold fast, be steady
Should the master come unexpected
Find us with orders still neglected
We then could have but one plea,
'Master we've neglected thee'
One chance more, let's act like men
With this entreaty I drop my pen".

As a rhymester he did literally drop his pen, for he died on 26th September, 1905 after a few day's illness, aged sixty-seven. Shortly before his death, he estimated that, during his twenty-eight years service as Bellman, he had walked over seventy thousand miles and had given six hundred thousand 'cries'.

It was a fitting tribute that the city mace-bearers, who had been associated with Childerhouse, attended the funeral in uniform as bearers. On September 28th so great was the popularity of this cheery soul, that an 'enormous crowd of sympathisers' congregated on the funeral route and at the cemetery.

"Well do I remember Childerhouse whose personality is so delightfully described. I can recall his nasal twang especially at the athletic sports held on Newmarket Road cricket ground. In announcing the results of the events and in other ways, he was wont to distinguish himself at this annual gathering."

Eastern Daily Press
Letters to the Editor
Phillip Soman, London

"Giles heard the voice while passing through Norwich on his way to London and this is what he said of it:-
As we got near the city I heard a most 'mazing loud voice, afore I could see anybody, that saamed to be telling the paaple all the news o' the day. I say to myself "Ye'd du well to kaap the birds off the whate in our fifty acre". Presently I seed a little chap wi' gold letters on his cap goin' along so quick that I thow't he must be on the Quaan's sarvice, and he comes up to our waggon and he say, "Daily Press, Gentlemen? Mornin Paaper, Gentlemen? All the news o' the day, only one penny".
"Well I say to myself, He's a smart little chap. I'll have a punnor o' 'im, it'll du to wrop suffin in if 'twont du for nor'n else".

A Norwich Celebrity.
'Childerhouse The
Bellman'
(Giles Trip To London, by
The Village Schoolmaster
Published by Jarrold &
Sons)

(sketches in dialect)

His first official announcement was made on behalf of the late Alderman Howlett, and was to the effect that the Band of the 5th (Royal Irish) Lancers would play in the skating rink that evening. As sword bearer and toastmaster he has had to wait upon royalty and the Prince and Princess of Wales, to say nothing of such minor fry as the Duke and Duchess of York, the Duke and Duchess of Connaught, etc. may almost said to be acquaintances of his. His duties lead him to all parts of the city and on one occasion at least they placed him in an awkward predicament. It was on that never to be forgotten Sunday when the Wensum o'erleaped it's banks and carried death and destruction through the low lying parts of the city. The Bellman was sent into the flooded district to announce that shelter would be provided in certain places for those who were driven from home by rising waters. While making his announcement from a coign of vantage afforded by a plank, he was suddenly precipitated into the torrent that was rushing past Gildencroft. Notwithstanding this ducking, the brave little man completed his round with his message of mercy before he went home to bed.

Mr. Roland Walker — co-director of a Norwich photographer's business says that one of his earliest jobs was photographing Billy Childerhouse,
"He was one of the quaintest little figures I have ever seen" says Mr. Walker.
"He had side whiskers, humorous eyes and was always most energetic".

Eastern Evening News
29th September, 1948

"Sir Jonathan Mardle's article on Childerhouse the Bellman gave me such pleasure for I know him quite well. It also brought back to me a very pleasant memory in which Childerhouse took part in what I think was the first "talkie" ever seen in Norwich. This is what happened:-
When Poole's myriorama was in session at the old Victoria Hall at the bottom of Bridewell Alley, they took a moving picture of Childerhouse delivering one of his famous cries at Howlett's Corner. When it was shown on the screen at Victoria Hall they had Childerhouse at the back and the timing was perfect. As I was standing by his side and in rather confined space the ringing of the bell and his powerful voice almost deafened me, but it was perfect — far better than the canned voice of the 'talkies' today".

Eastern Daily Press
Letter to the Editor,
by A.E. Amond, Hingham

Eastern Daily Press
Wednesday,
3rd November, 1926
Dr. Beverley's
Recollections Overstand.

"Your contributions re the Bellman of Norwich have revived many pleasant memories — never shall I forget the morning when we who lived in St. Giles were startled by a stentorian voice, "Daily Press, Daily Press" and a little man was to be seen running rapidly through the street. He was easily recognised by form and voice as Childerhouse the Bellman. Through my front door was thrown the birthday number of the 'Eastern Daily Press'. I have taken it ever since. Childerhouse and his wife — a giantess compared to him — I knew well — they were my patients. I had a great regard for them both. They kept a pork butcher's shop in Ber Street and brought up a large family. Childerhouse was easily (facile princeps) as a Town Crier and when his voice was silenced by death the city felt his loss. Why was this useful and picturesque functionary given up? Those of us who recently listened on the wireless to a competition between existing Bellmen must have regretted that Norwich was not represented.

Eastern Evening News
5th March, 1968

". . . Bellman Childerhouse must have been one of the first Town Criers to have had false teeth and to have allowed his picture to be used for 'commercial' such as we have on television nowadays. A pamphlet was issued by J.M. Imray, 25 St. Benedicts with a picture of a gummy Bellman before being fitted with

Imray's false teeth and a picture of a much better looking Bellman afterwards. Testimonials on the back of the pamphlet range from 1898 until 1906 and all speak highly of Mr. Imray's false teeth supplied at 3s.0d. and 4s.6d. per tooth and 5s.0d. for the finest quality.

1906/1912   Harry Moulton   Bellman
Following the death of Childerhouse the city committee received nineteen applications for the office of Bellman. Three applicants were selected and they, together with the committee, adjourned to Chapel Field Gardens, where the vocal powers of the three men were tested. Mr. Harry Moulton, then of 66 Coburg Street, was adjudged to be the most 'stentorian shouter' and he was appointed.
According to 'Fisher's Almanac' for 1906 which published a portrait and a short account of Moulton, he was 'at one time a drummer in the band of No.1 corps of the local Salvation Army'.
In 1907 Moulton received a new bell bearing the city arms with the date 1907 and lettered W.R.C. Howlett, Mayor. This bell is now preserved at the Guildhall. So far as is known Moulton did not issue any addresses. In May 1912 the city committee decided to terminate his appointment in view of the disuse by the public of the services of the Bellman.

Eastern Daily Press
27th October, 1926

Eastern Daily Press
31st May, 1929

Harry Moulton, last of the Norwich Bellmen, has died in St. Helen's Hospital, Norwich, at the age of seventy-three. Moulton, who was a fine figure of a man, succeeded the famous Childerhouse in the post and held it until it was finally extinguished. After the end of his Bellmanship, Moulton was a buyer of antiques until two years ago, when he entered St. Helen's Hospital. He leaves a son and daughter.

Ancient and Honourable Guild of Town Criers Records.

1985 David Anthony Bullock Town Crier Appointed 1985.

Uniform — Red Coat, black cuffs, with gold braid, red waiscoat with gold braid, black tricorn hat with gold braid and ostrich feather, white lace jabot and cuffs, black knee breeches, white stockings and black buckle shoes.

He is a member and serjeant of the Ancient and Honourable Guild of Town Criers and in 1992 had the honour to be elected Chairman of the Guild.

In his capacity as Town Crier, he is involved in civic ceremonies in the city of Norwich. He also attends at charity functions and 'cries' commercially. He has taken part in many Town Crier competitions, both in this country and abroad and has been Champion Crier several times.

In 1989, following the tradition of local Criers/Bellmen, he issued a Christmas address and added a final verse to one of a past Norwich Bellman, William Childerhouse's, 1887 Christmas address poem on Bellmanship:-

All past Bellmen can now rejoice
Who woke this city with bell and
voice
And now have crossed on Charon's
Ferry.
Such men as Buxton, Basse and Berry.
Of others too we remember now
Gobet, Empson and Eastaugh.
In late Victoria times, we see
William Childerhouse made his mark
By shouting daily on his rounds
And rarely after dark.
From 1905 the position lapsed
For many a long year.
But in 1986 a Town Crier did appear
For messages now, to be called and
shouted
Around the city centre
Of commerce, civic and tourism
And bidding good people to enter.
Town Crier or Bellman, it's a very
proud post
With a history of Bellman of whom
one can boast.

Nathaniel Eastaugh

29

Nathaniel Eastaugh

James Berry

James Berry

Josiah Berry

Norwich. The Old City Bellman.

William Childerhouse

Death of Bellman Childerhouse.

NORWICH loses a popular and active official, and an original public character, by the death of Mr. William Childerhouse, the city bellman. For 28 years he carried the bell, and bore the Corporation sword on State occasions; and it is estimated that he walked about 70,000 miles whilst fulfilling the duties of town crier. Mr. Childerhouse was a born bellman — with the proper official mien, a sonorous voice which rivalled the brazen tones of his bell, and a quaint style which well fitted his ancient office. He was the most familiar figure in our city streets; and although he lived by "crying", he always preserved a genial and smiling aspect. Visitors regarded him as one of the "sights" of old Norwich; and his portrait has been sent to all parts of the world by thousands on picture postcards. His decease has created general sympathy and regret; for we are assured that in the town-crier department we shall not see his like again. However, a very capable successor has been appointed in the person of Mr. Harry Moulton, who will undoubtedly uphold the traditions of an office which goes back for centuries.

Copyright.

By the way, the long line of Norwich bellmen can be traced back for generations; and the following list may prove interesting :-

1793—Nathaniel Eastaugh.
1804—John Buckle.
1805—Nathaniel Eastaugh.
1810—Anthony Bailey.
1813—Robert Juby.
1835—Nathaniel Eastaugh.
1856—James Berry.
1857—Josiah Berry.
1877—William Childerhouse.
1905—Harry Moulton.

THE LATE BELLMAN'S LAST VERSE.

There was something almost prophetic in Bellman Childerhouse's last verse, which was written for his annual address published last Christmas, and which runs as follows :-

We know not, and we cannot tell
For whom this year will toll the bell.
Many have gone whom we thought
In this year would still have wrought.
The same old watch word "Be ye ready!"
On Life's seas hold fast, be steady;

Should the Master come unexpected,
Find us with orders still neglected,
We then could have but one plea
"Master, we have neglected Thee"
One chance more, let's act like men;
With this entreaty I drop my pen.

William Childerhouse

Fisher's Almanac and Annual, 1906.

THE NEW BELLMAN.

Copyright.

Harry Moulton

It would have been a matter of regret to many citizens if the ancient office of bellman had been allowed to disappear; for the office is well nigh as old as the Mayoralty, and in recent years the duties have been brought up-to-date in order to meet modern needs. It was satisfactory therefore that the Corporation signified its intention to appoint a successor to Mr. Childerhouse, and that more than a dozen applicants sought the post. Three were selected, and their vocal capabilities were tested in Chapel Field with the result that Mr. Harry Moulton was adjudged to be the most stentorian shouter, and secured the appointment. The selection appears to be an excellent one; and the new bellman will soon be seen in the glory of his official uniform and gold laced hat. Mr. Moulton's stalwart figure is well known in the city, and he was at one time drummer in the band of the No.1 Corps of the local Salvation Army. Let us hope that he may wield the bell as long and as successfully as his predecessor.

Fisher's Almanac and Annual, 1906.

THE NORWICH BELLMAN & HIS DOG PRINCE. COPYRIGHT.

Harry Moulton

David A. Bullock

GREAT YARMOUTH
Norfolk

1349   Bellmen

"In 1349, Isabel, wife of Jeffrey De Fordele, bequeathed 'to the two Bellmen of the town of Great Yarmouth and their successors for the time being for ever, sixpence of annual rent on condition that they celebrate the anniversary of me and Thomas Sydler and ring for our souls according to the manner and said custom of the said towne'.

(The Thomas Sidler here mentioned was one of the persons summoned in 1340)

(De essendo coram concillio)

Manship's History of Great Yarmouth Edited by C.J. Palmer Vol. 2 Page 296

1465   Bellman

"Bellman to cover images of saints in Great Yarmouth church during Lent".

Page 119

1603   Common Crier

"Upon Tweisdaie 9th October, the common Crier of the town cried, "Oysters to be sold" without our consent, for which we reprehended him and sent to the partie that made sale thereof that he might not lawfully doe it without our consent, who thereupon sent unto us a pech of the said oysters for a tast and prayed our allowance to sell the residue, to which we assented.

Page 76 – from 'Relation' by John Coyne of Hastings and John Tooke of Dover on a visit to Great Yarmouth during the Freefair there in 1603

16??   John Gates   Bellman

1644   John Golding   Bellman
4th October 1644 — John Golding chosen — ? of John Gates — Bellman

1689   William Aldridge   Bellman
Appointed 22nd October 1689

1691   Thomas Lingwood   Bellman
Elected 29th January 1691

1691   Jeremiah Hanton   Bellman
Appointed 28th July 1691

1695   Bellman
'Ordered that the Chamberlain buy the Bellman a new coat, breeches, hat, stockings at the corporation charge'

1697   John Dunn   Bellman
'Upon the petition of John Dunn it is ordered that he be continued Bellman of this burgh during the pleasure of this assembly and the Chamberlains are ordered to cloath him with a coat, and breeches, a hat and stockings and a new belt for his bell.

1703/23   William Smith   Bellman
'William Smith of this town, cordwainer, elected Bellman for this town, during the pleasure of this assembly and he keeping himself sober and coming to the Church of England

every Sunday forenoon and afternoon and it is further ordered that the Chamberlains provide, allow and deliver unto Mr. Smith such like the same sort of livery clothes and apparel as his predessors had.

1723/46   Hall Turner   Bellman   *Volume 4 Page 91*
Appointed instead of William Smith (deceased)
The Chamberlains are ordered to   *Page 131*
provide a new livery for the Bellman, his old one being very ragged and torn.

1746   Also this assembly think proper to   *Page 295*
discharge Hall Turner from his office of Bellman in this corporation. He is by this assembly discharged accordingly.

1747   Thomas Bowles   Bellman   *Page 301*
Appointed Bellman instead of Hal Turner discharged.

1747   David Bull   Bellman   *Page 304*
Elected Bellman instead of Thomas Bowles discharged.

1762   William Gidney   Bellman   *Volume 5 Page 77*

1762/74   Phineas Grimble   Bellman   *Page 77*
Elected Bellman in the room of William Gidney, deceased.

Page 133/4

1774/78   Richard Harridance   Bellman
Appointed Bellman instead of Phineas
Grimble discharged.

Page 148

1778/84   Thomas Steward   Bellman
Appointed Bellman instead of Richard
Harridance deceased.

Page 200

1784/86   Samuel Bowles   Bellman
Appointed Bellman 5th January 1785

Page 226/7

1785 — Mr. Mayor reports to this assembly
that Samuel Bowles, the Bellman, who
had by him, been suspended for
misbehaving, having himself
acknowledged his offence and humbly
petitioned to be restored to the office,
the Mayor, on his promise of future
good behaviour returned him the bell,
which this assembly approves of. He
resigned in 1786.

Page 234

1786/1808   Josiah Curtis   Bellman
Appointed Bellman 8th September
1786 instead of Samuel Bowles resigned.

*Palmer's Perlustrations
of Great Yarmouth*

"In the second house on the north side of
Row No. 32, resided in the last century
Josiah Curtis, who filled the office of
Town Crier or Bellman, as he was
usually called for thirty-two years. He
was appointed in 1786, Samuel Bowles
his predecessor, having been suspended
for 'ill behaviour' in the previous year.
He was the last who wore the ancient
dress, consisting of a long loose blue

cloth coat, open at the neck and fastened round the waist by a leather girdle, knee breeches, white stockings and shoes with large buckles. Over his dress was slung a leather case containing his big bell, the strap being adorned by a silver escutcheon of the town arms. On his head he wore a three cornered hat.

He was an officer of the Corporation and on state occasions carried a huge staff with a silver knob. Curtis had a stentorian voice and pompous manner. He prefixed every 'cry', however trivial the subject, with 'O Yes! O Yes! O Yes!' (a corruption of the ancient Oyez — hear ye — the usual prelude to a proclamation in the olden time) and concluded with 'God Save the King'. He was the son of Josiah Curtis, hairdresser and parish sexton (an odd mixture of trades) who died in 1803 aged eighty-nine, by Elizabeth his wife, who died in 1799, aged eighty-six. Robert, another son, a cordwainer in Middlegate Street, died in 1831 in his eightieth year. The family are said to have greatly impoverished themselves by their excessive love of beer, which habit, however, does not seem to have shortened their lives. Curtis himself was believed capable of imbibing an unlimited quantity during his daily rounds. He never failed to pour a small portion of the liquor upon the ground if in the open air, but probably did not know that by so doing he observed an old pagan custom, dating from a very remote period, of making a propitiatory offering to mother earth.*

*The custom still lingers at the doors of country ale houses (Teste me ipso)

When he had drained a mug to the bottom he would look into it and facetiously observe that he saw Moll Thompson's mark — M.T. — (empty). (He sang the old song:-
'Oh ale! Ab alendo, thou liquor of life! That I had but a mouth as big as a whale!
For mine is too little, to tell the least tittle!
Of all the fine things that belong to good ale!)

Bellmen were probably subject to great inducements to drink.
Curtis died in 1818 aged seventy-four. There is a small full length portrait of him in his official dress by Swanborough, in the possession of Francis Worship, Esquire, from which the annexed engraving is taken.

Portrait now in the Elizabethan House Museum South Quay, Great Yarmouth.

Palmer's Perlustrations Volume I Page 80

Formerly it was the custom, when a husband was dissatisfied with the extravagances of his wife, to have her cried down at the cross; in later times the announcement was made by the Bellman during his daily round.

1808/	Richard Paul	Bellman	*Great Yarmouth Assembly Book*
1819/29	Joseph Ablitt	Bellman	

Appointed 1st September 1819

1834	Richard Paul	Bellman	*Information from an 1834 address*
1843/44	James Miller	Bellman	*Information from 1843 and 1844 addresses*
1867/75	Henry Bayes Thompson	Bellman	*Yarmouth Almanac 1867*
1875/1901	Henry Thompson	Bellman	

Josiah Curtis

Richard Paul